THERE'S AN EXCESS AT THE HEART OF BEING THAT'S WILD

T0159878

TODD
SWIFT

THERE'S AN EXCESS AT THE HEART OF BEING THAT'S WILD

AN EYEWEAR
SPECIAL
PAMPHLET

First published in 2019
by Eyewear Publishing Ltd
Suite 333, 19-21 Crawford Street
Marylebone, London W1H 1PJ
United Kingdom

Typeset with graphic design by Edwin Smet
Photos by Todd Swift

ISBN 978-1-912477-90-6

WWW.EYEWEARPUBLISHING.COM

i.m. I.M. Pei

my mother's favourite architect,
with fond memories of the first building
of his I saw with her

TABLE OF CONTENTS

The poem is the central place for an affirmation of the power fantasy has over reality, or rather, seeks to possess. The poem is a perverse realm, where all the humiliations, weaknesses and disappointments of reality are overturned, subverted, or challenged. The poem is made of linguistic statements – verbal claims – that cannot and will not be tested by reason, science, law or other institutions of morality or social sanction. The poem stands somewhat aside from the psalm, the hymn, the prayer, the vow, the promise – so-called good words. The poem says what it wants, when it wants, and its claims are beyond the power of power.

Poetry is not magic, or a spell. It is not about enacting actual power or transformation over the real world. It establishes a separate realm, an alternative world of its own, in order to sidestep reality. It does not perform miracles – it renders the miraculous redundant. The poem is precisely the polymorphous perverse play of the child. A poem is always aware of its status as supreme escape mechanism, as the superior enabler of the forbidden, the unsayable, the bizarre, the weird, the sublime and beautiful.

After religion, only the poem can reply to the twin facts of death and decay with any authority. Its reply is: *yes, you can kill us in the real world – you have dominion in the realm of facticity – but no one has more sway or dominion over the fictive, the unreal, the dreamt, the desired, and the imagined, than the poem.* The poem sets up a rival court, a rival kingdom, and its rule is unchallenged. Poetry is the irrational king and queen. Poetry acts not by denying the terrible awful laws of science and reality, however, but by revelling in describing them, railing against them, mocking them – inexhaustibly, obsessively worrying at, picking at, the wounds of real pain and ageing, death and loss.

Like a horror story, the poem's power is in its unflinching gaze at the worst that can happen, and its haughty refusal to quail. The poem may lament and stamp its feet, or soar above, the grave scene, but it never denies the grave scene occurs. It is just that it occurs in a world that has poetry in it also, the eternal enemy of law, the final riposte. Poetry's perverse power is aesthetic, ironic, and bound in play – it believes that just as science and reason rely on rules and structure, so too do the formal fixations and options of poetry set up an alternate framework, an oppositional mode of experiencing being.

Non-fiction is non-fixation. Poetry cannot stop, it must repeat, like an impulse, an itch that must be scratched, endlessly. So long as there are death and endings, there will be poetry. For poetry you could say sex, but sex is too private, personal and ephemeral – the poem as an object is a fetish with more solidity than any mortal object's body. The poem replaces the sexual body as the new site of erotic majesty. In the poem, even more than in the dream, or fantasy, one is omnipotent – because the poem is never exhausted by physical release. It surpasses even the transcendent ecstasies.

It's chaos from the top down –
Stereophonics

The uncontrollable mystery
on the bestial floor –
WB Yeats

GLOVES FOR MIMI

One way to define a futile gesture is to say art
Might be the best fit, just the thing for that part;
Go to *La Boheme* and listen to the failing Mimi;
It's easy to see them going to buy her a flimsy

Excuse for a cure – gloves to warm icy hands
That won't ever heat up again – image of plans
Doomed by the imperious march of time's army;
Poetry is like that, too, if only a bit less smarmy –

Watch the way it peels on the layers, as if saying
Creativity was the likeness of successful praying –
But the stiff libretto of life translated from Italian
Into dying sings a few octaves below salvation;

No form of art can be more than leather on skin;
It's a kind of sugar to coat the futility we're in;
Even the meanest words are melodic Puccini
Brushing up against time's morbid realities.

So, was it better to offer the ailing flirty cutey
A pricey piece of clothing, a bargain of beauty,
Or ignore her moans of displeasure in their garret?
I write always to burn my papers for any vedette

Of stage, street or tavern who needs a little heat;
Any who can even briefly assist the dying with a treat
Must essay that feat. We're all in bohemian poverty
At the end of days; go give your best gloves to Mimi.

COLDEST DAY OF THE YEAR

Frost on the playing field,
a lone hockey player (grass, not ice)
tries out her stick, listlessly,
exposed knees freezing; a vision
of winter in modern Britain

facing off, 1 against 27
in the struggle of our time –
to break away from a union
that has only yielded bounty
so far. Something in us

resists control, boundaries, even
binding laws and customs.
The end of January in W9
is bright as a penny – shining
sun on the recently pruned trees.

What is with the English
and their gardening?
The apocalypse could be coming,
they'd be out with the shears,
kneeling to nurture bloody roses.

BONNIE AND CLYDE

the solution is to die,
I miss you, I miss you wide

and narrow, in the day
and tomorrow, after

you have left, before
you come; a dream,

a sorrow, a knife
in the ribs and a gun

under the pillow,
we kill for love

of robbery, we steal
the love of others;

in motels
we escape, barely,

our terrible mistakes;
I miss you, I miss your

body as it lies down
and rises, every way

we walk together,
across the field,

to the bank, packing heat
in that hat.

BLOOD CYCLOTRON REPORT

I T-logiced back to witness Cain,
Invisibly in micro-craft hovering,
Monitoring to halt the first murder,
Source of the bloodletting spring,
Cats in the corn arresting the vermin,
When he lurched forward, human,
Lusty with two-fisted envying,
I stepped in, with my robot wingmen,
Fully-armed hellfire drones buzzing,
Abel freezing as his brother's stone
Hit pause in the crackling air,
The second of seeing red before green;
I saw the universal spiral, unspooling

From this spoiling initiating atrocity –
How from the origin story of killing
A cycle broke its frame, to a never-ending
Series, cruel on cruel, sheet to screen,
Sullying with self-same staining, a sinning
Bigger than nature, empire, war-winning;
It would take a momentary correction
To wipe this terrible slate clean.
So, then, hit Alpha-key, set in motion a whirring;
Blew Cain to smithereens, scatter
Of hate across the sand; his sibling unfortunate
Collateral crossfire statistical error malfunctioning;
Zipped to 2119, unseen, barely gone.

HORSE

Confessions start with a crime, which starts
with a Russian novel; there are gamblers
who die when they run out of red balls, or black,
if I have my roulette references in order;

it's a tall one, trying to formulate a reasonable
response to mania that kills; oh yeah, back
to the confessional, that little box of lies,
or half-truths, and what are half-lives in radiation law?

I'm confused because split like an LP, remember those?
Vinyl is back, so are schizoid conditions
in the human test tube that's the soul.
Souls begin in Moscow, with Fyodor.

Why is there no band called The Fyodors?
There must be. Google. Poems no longer exist
separately from online. We're tangled up
just as we burst apart. The breaking heart

is a signal from splintering ice when the ship
breaks the floes. It's cold in Montreal where
they bury the snow-fort boys. I quit smoking heroin
when the night nurse said I was dead already.

I can't quit one particular girl. She's an anime speedball.
It's all descending like a Tupolev TU-144. Damn fast.
Confession doesn't help if you're unwilling to change.
AA only works if you've hit the bottom of the pool, where

all the kids drown. I'm on the surface of my affections,
I am floating in a world of imminent destruction.
Cheap romance paperbacks featuring nurses can't thrill when you're
injecting the true shit; I'm in Russian novels.

POEMS ON UNORIGINAL THEMES FOUR:
POOL HALLS

There's one with Fats and one with Slim,
one with you, and one with him,
but they all have tables scuffed and green
like money is in Charleston, where

this particular ball and cue are,
which I stand behind, as if a great idea
I would die for; and the others stand around
because I've taken every other down

into the pockets like a demon
hauling souls off the surface of the planet;
I am playing like a very smart comet;
each shot is German-engineered

by way of St-Lambert. Each time
I don't fail someone flinches.
You measure life in lined-up inches
that connect to a hand, guided

by the best eye you can manage
in the gunmetal blue smoke of the air
that hovers like palm trees napalmed
with sweat and fear. Nixon

is President, it is that sort of year;
and a lot of boys are over there.
Canadian, cavalier, thin as a poker,
I have no card dragging me to quarrel

with rice-eating peasants.
Finches, pheasants, swifts, cats, voles,
all creatures crawl or soar, or burrow,
but only one creature stretches

across a table while alive,
in order to move an object
to strike another object
to impress a girl in a summer dress

leaning at the bar, half-elsewhere.
This is my sonnet and my portrait,
this racking up of one game,
then another, as fins circle,

dissipate. It gets late
and then it gets more than late;
morning and a barber come
to shave us back into the day.

We play because born to play;
and because outside
it is July, and there is a war,
and we won't die so quickly this way.

Not so long as I lose a bit every hour;
power must never impress
too completely, but pocket,
like a sly trick, its ultimate prowess.

She has left; the fan circles; the cigars
are stale; soldiers killed; beer flat;
and my life has just begun.
Tomorrow or yesterday, twenty-one,

I always bend and straighten, complete
in one fell swoop a more perfect motion,
as if the spheres were instruments
that played in my blood; I am not good,

that is the name for also-rans.
I began a week ago, and will go on so long
as they still come with wads, a glimmer,
a wink and hope; they want to defeat

a force of nature, like some ride waves
manfully with boards. Let them come.
Bring your children and women to see.
There is always a friend I won't meet.

A skirt I don't chase. I am pinioned
here on this table as if dissected,
a dead man being opened
to solve a crime. I can clear

the whole shebang in one turn.
How did I learn? I had a father.
He was the pope of this small world,
and for him it was never a game,

it was the field of torment
where a guy is tested, usually fails.
I break, and it is all sails on smooth ocean,
green motion; I do not sink, I never sink,

what should not sink, until time to fall
to save my neck from beatings,
pay some back, catch some winks,
or sex's brief grind, or earn some mortal

experience. How it feels to be imperfect.
My name? You knew it from the start.
It says it right there, on the wood, man.
Peradon. 1885. Pleased to meet.

POEMS ON UNORIGINAL THEMES FIVE:
UNREQUITED LOVE

Have you read *De Profundis*?
It doesn't rhyme with profound,
more with a kiss. Wilde wrote it,
in the clink. Suffering, as he did.
Love lies, and kills in droves.
It hacks and hacks and saws
and mows down great swathes of roses
and humans in the way of those.

Swinburne too was picked apart
by hungers of the body
somehow connected to the art
of being chastised, without
being truly culpable, in roles
of being a bad boy
with a very naughty part to play
in the troubling closet of the heart.

Poets tend to end with a pistol
to the brain; or throw their
heroines like pearls beneath
a very moving train; alone
of all the animals that hunt
for pleasure, is the artist
in tremendous vascular pain;
love rains down its blows

like gross bodily harm
had been paid for and delivered
in the name of all that is unholy

in the book of demands.
You can smash the irreparable
but nothing is quite as clear
as the nuclear device of gutting
the lover you leave with a letter

open at the line about someone else.
O I could complain, but then
again, too morose and a bit plain.
Sex is an eye rhyme with the hex
that makes the lack of it unsweet;
once tasted, no sugar else will do;
you are the tea that suits me, you.
Obsession is the result

of hocus pocus and a clear lack
of focus on other boys and girls to do.
Here in this grime of elsewhere
and after I have no view. Bricked up
and abandoned like any factory
whose engines have been foreclosed
I idle to rust, dust and endlessness
without purpose any more, or true

voice, or valance; all is skewed
and facing the wall that spits back
a bitter taste of uselessness.
What happens to you now, and nightly,
drives me like a coach through a nuthouse
into tatters of confused sobs and sips;
I die at the gutter of your refusing lips.
I could write for ever, it has an inkwell

at its base does loss of love, the ache
spills more language than all the jewels

in heaven's crown; I'm jilted badly here,
I'm thrown around like marbles, you're cruel,
but give me a break – that is unfair.
I led you on, left you alone, for fear.
You deserved everything I did not give.
I grieve how much without me you live.

OPPENHEIMER'S LAMENT

After the credits, I sit dumbfounded
in the velvet cinema, as complete

as any film noir trauma can ever be;
it's more than over, like the cigarette

that evokes a cloud even in its dying state;
embers have a bad habit of lingering;

call it memory, call it fate,
or a mixed-up cocktail of hate-love;

I'm in a state of arousal, sure,
but in the way a hanged man is.

It's done but circles back, like life
in death, or certain birds of prey;

I'm over everything but the dream girl
who took my heart like winnings

at Baccarat. I'm radiating an energy
not usually associated with morbidity.

I've lost the right – one I never had –
to lay a claim to her scent, her arms.

I'm so enamoured at the testing site,
where goggles are worn to ward

off the blinding more-than-sun
of this imploding structure that burns stars,

I'm divine with it; rotten to the molten core.
I am cooling slowly, over eons,

but still have her burnt-across-shadow
to pacify my hunger on the radiant floor.

ON THE DEATH OF KARL LAGERFELD

I've come to accept that if Lagerfeld can die,
So too will I. It's just evolutionary medicine.
In fact, according to George C. Williams,
Ageing is passed on because the fittest procreate

With the best genetic aspects upfront, in youth;
We're built for the sprint, not the marathon;
The blind watchmaker doesn't give a damn
What happens once we're spent swimmers,

Having dropped a big litter. We're baby machines
In all but name. This is what's subversive
About the narcissism of contemporary fashion.
To be shallow, and self-focused, flamboyant,

A leather-clad cat-owner, a glove-fetishist,
A designer of things that have no reproductive
Value – well, that's more than nihilistic fun.
It's a statement, that humans can rise above

The laws of mere concupiscence and copulation.
Though I suppose beautiful clothing is a mating
Ritual, and hence, folded into the copulative process.
It's hard to escape the idea that chance is by design,

Or we're made by chance, except, chance is no thing.
It's a description of a process, not a seeing hand;
To be random or unplanned cannot explain style's hold;
There's an excess at the heart of being that's wild.

ICY DAYS IN THE EASTERN TOWNSHIPS

This is the sort of January blue light
day that has no need for perversity,
it reminds me of the simpler times
of ice and snow and grandparents,
in Melbourne, Quebec, when, minus
twenty, you could see the ice floes
in the river, and slow trains across
the iron bridge, past the Wales Home,
for the very old. Those weren't really
simpler times, I suppose – sex
and murder, guilt and compromise
still happened; as did debt and loss;
hate, and faithlessness; despair –
and farmers hung in scraped barns
to be found by young daughters;
wars, and Fords breaking down;
rust, slow Maple sap; a wolf coming
from the mountains, half-starved;
not simpler, but still, less complex;
nothing that occurred then
was ever shared instantly everywhere;
commented on; judged wanting;
despised; ignored; living wasn't
digital; it spilled like oats, loosely
from the bag of days, and you bent
to scoop up what you could,
and when you paused in the frost
to catch your breath physical
as an axe forcing open the blue air,
you felt you were a part of a world,
of words, and images, things unseen,

far bigger, and mostly somewhere else,
and often, never visited, never lent.
It was the quiet of smaller places;
the lack of encroachment, a chance
this back-woods would remain untaken;
the greater battles passing over,
like in the Bible when that danger
didn't stop at certain painted doors,
Richmond's winter calm among blizzards.

JUDGING INSTAGRAM POETRY

You can be cynical and superior only so long
Before succumbing to the inherent pathos
Of the tortured songs of the almost-young,
Whose tornadoes of despair appear to be those
Instigated by the climate of our digital rag-shop
And the sheer alpine sloping decline of politics;
They write at times simply, badly, but won't stop;
It's their pain, protest, passion, that sticks.
It makes me question the very basis of my PhD:
Style in poetry is the apex of achievement.
For these bards, expression of themselves is key,
Their sincerest heartfelt words are meant.
Now poets don't want to outdo our old canonical masters,
The work's instant magic, they're self-made spell-casters.

IDENTITY THEFT

One separates from one's self
Like albums on Spotify, all singles now;
And no one owns any stuff anymore,
Not even themselves – it is all rented,

On cloud-based shelves. I'm coming
Apart, no point holding on much longer,
I'm in sync with a breaking world.
Nervous it was once called, this eventuality,

A decline as precipitous as the cards down
That once housed their suits, their royalty.
I'm the face of facelessness, now;
Staring out at the collapse of day, called night.

Don't give yourself a fright, just binge
On stolen TV. I feel sick at hearts,
And minds. I'm a divided notion, voting down
The middle of my best intentions. Sick

In mind, sick in soul, uncurable, all of it, really.
Don't go out, stay in. Wear the clothes left on
After you've removed your property
Of all the clutter that made you your own worst

Enemy; or friend. In the end, things get
In the way of getting away from our selves;
They define what we thought held value, like gold,
When value mattered, was tangible. The old

World is being swept away, in such few waves.
It's a relentless time, it feels oncoming, rushing,
It's weaponised rapidity, a silver bullet to a forehead;
A diamond-pointed stylus loving vinyl for irony.

There's no money in it, no one spends anymore,
They barely earn, they complain instead.
I'm institutionally useless, writing whiteness
Across an unhappy screen; there's no place

In this placeless domain; I'm abandoned.
I am a factory rusting; a buried pet.
There's a memory of something melancholy,
A profound earlier time, lying under the ground.

In this wide present, its flat and even cinema
Is uncannily housed at home; audiences isolate.
The great reveal their small foibles, sins as evils.
No one forgives anymore, it's all judgement, gavels.

I have a pounding head, and a suspicion I'm to blame.
I'm not human, and I cannot remember my code name.
I'll identify the bicycles, the bridges, the cars, the traffic
Lights – now let me in, I'm not a robot, I'm problematic.

CREDO 2019

I write poems for men and women
Who love each other, and other combinations,

I write poems for adults of all kinds,
Of each description, I cannot adjudicate

Who is Gary, who is Kate, who marries
At which kissing gate. I plant no apples,

I tear no corn. I give no council; deliver
The unborn cautiously. I write out of hate

That wants to taper to a colder flame;
I'm openly broken and seeking a claim

Over a parcel of land in Canaan.
I forgive nothing but the sins of fire.

I pour a gourd of spring water warily.
I have little water and must go far soon.

They say it is auspicious when the winter moon
Is full. I think all that is ripe is terrifying.

The world's in riot like a summer day.
We murder the picnic as if it was a goat.

Take my coat, and nail the report to the walls.
Please be good and dangerous to each other

On a passionate mission to delay
The unenviable stop of your single occupancy.

Brutalise the air and slap the sun like a fly.
Be bigger than anything you find in your way.

I write for you who can become adult eventually
No matter how long you take growing to there.

Poems can be everything, laws for art
Are rules for a boundless game, foolish as bird

Catching with ropes – works fitfully, often fails
And falls. Birds in a tangled net

Are not the sky's ruckus, its rich finds.
We can bring down less than we aim for.

Aspire to get there, rather than grab it down.
I write poems seriously, without pretension,

Knowing they are no more read
Than a river stream pays notice of its pebbles,

Those glistening momentary stones,
Rushed along on the raucous natural ructions.

POEM FOR MY WIFE IN WINTER

I saw the future end of my life
one Sunday in February
when the storm winds blew
across the island,

and I knew then
I'd rue the day I betrayed
all our careful vows,
spread out in sunshine early

in our lives together,
when we feared the weather
might turn against us,
but were mostly spared;

and I will regret the hours
of self-pleasure and waste,
the lurid pastimes, idle games,
competitions and coin tosses,

manoeuvrings, jostling,
searches and envies;
I should have knelt each day
and been so glad for the cold

and the worst rains; my aches
and your pains; our barren
bed and desert plains.
The sun parches, the water dries;

the seas have lost deep music,
and the mountains are small.
But it was a greatness
to be conceived and mounted,

to be delivered and saved,
to live and be educated,
to read and talk, to dance
and walk, to partake

of wine and your kiss.
I was an idiot constantly,
I was remiss. I had religion
and fervour but no will to refrain;

I sang like a melting winter
with its flooding gains,
I was joyous over the wrong things;
I brought incorrigible gifts

to barbarian kings;
I ate poison, drank meat.
I should have stayed with you
and wrapped my arms tight,

and kept you my own.
I should have guarded our doors
with a flame and a sword,
and a sneering word

for devils of my own design.
I desired to decline as an art,
but misunderstood poetry;
I took apart my life

like a shell to eat the softest parts;
in the process I devoured
the kindness of your beating heart.
God forgive me as I die.

Please let me go to heaven
if only for the briefest interval,
to see my only wife.
I wish to meet her steady gaze

and kneel and bow,
weep unutterably late praise.

BLACK SPRING

Radio, live transmission
On the stream, and Black Spring press
Being unpacked. It's a bleak, thin
Anticipation of some light, there's a slim
Sun out there, victim of Britain's dithering;
Indecision and joyless division

Marking the UK, a chaos in crisis,
And the blackest sun antipodean
And within too many; hats and gove
On each badly-tattooed hand,
As if nothingness or plenitude
Stood around the back, waiting

To beat the shit out of winter, for boredom;
The planet as planet will survive, barely.
We're part of the general comedy of spring,
As unutterably undeserved as salvation;
As unlikely, and still, potential.
The kids with knives kill because they are sick,

Or are killed because the world spins
In increasingly social disarray;
We're bound by twisted algorithms,
Suffering us to come on to each other's sins;
We're being asked to prefer our perversity;
Perversely sending signals, like transmitters

Sewn into dolls by traffickers;
The trees blossoming in the cold-looking park,
They are all victims of happening

Amidst our temporal machinations,
The age of the human, as if that was
A good or fruitful thing; we're

A sort of anti-spring, darkening
The year with negation; there's hope,
The rhetoric of poetry demands at this stage;
Recurring thoughts of sacrifice, compassion.
In this spring at least there's a slope
Edging to regeneration.

SPRING EQUINOX, 2019

POEM FOR MY WIFE ON THE EVE OF
HER BIRTHDAY

A birthday in this Instagram age makes me
Want to be the main theme of your social page;
I photobomb the very day you were born,

Jump into the personal frame, happy to be
The central focus of your own latest age:
Forty-seven, six less than mine; that morn,

You arrived, and were the louder joy
You've remained ever since – not it's a boy!
But it's a bouncing laughing Irish girl!

I was of course premature, and Canadian.
Let's not spoil March Thirtieth with facts –
But it's only nine days before the Eighth of April.

The jostle is truly our unifying religion, we
Share being the bold brats known as Aries;
Butt heads in the daily, weekly, and annual ways

That roistering couples do. True, I am older,
Heavier of girth, and write far more poetry, yet
In other ways we're similar and evenly matched:

We're precisely the same medium height;
And both adore our black Bombay cat Suetonius.
You're blonde, blue-eyed, generally kind, and fun.

I'm the brown-eyed, dark-haired melancholy one.
I'm the burnt toast on which you spread honey.
I'm the hole in the pocket that lets fall out money.

It's entirely fine that you've continued to thrive
During a time of upheaving discontent in Britain
And the wider world. I'm glad to be your companion

As the whole process of living becomes more terrible.
As Yeats played upon paradox, that's also beautiful.
I am terrified of going it alone, so am eternally glad

You married me, then let me live with you in this pad.
Many returns, you deserve blessings because are good,
In the way love-names cut deep into still-growing wood.

MARCH 29, 2019

A MEDITATION ON APRIL FOOL'S DAY 2019

Literature is dangerous – Georges Bataille

Who walks in April sun like an ice display, to be chipped
At the party, will also age like brittle renunciations,
Bishops bitter over medieval quarrels, even ancient ones.
I am as shy as it is possible for a shady character to be,

This you and me I carry in my outmoded manner;
I was late to the flagellation, but it came, like a polar
Blast in the unconvincing summer. Winds shift, times
Crumble like a church fete when it begins to pelt down;

I am a man who has failed evolution's tests, my testes
Dysfunctional, the six-pound man no science rebuilt.
I do have what it takes to announce a kilt, I'm cocked
If empty of shells. Yes, the old complaint, my dear,

I'm sterile in all the wrong implements, a dire dentist.
That's not why being almost-fifty-three terrifies;
No day is duller than a Monday April Fool, at noon;
Jokes have dissipated, if any there were to be had.

Dad jokes even for the non-dads. My father's a memorable
Anecdote or three, a lost cause, his drinking troubles
No longer curable, or incurable, depending on your POV.
Half my family is in the cesspit, the charnel house,

But that's nothing compared to history's open graves.
Jesus saved me when I was a born again teen in 1983.
How's that worked out, eh? An arch-bishop gilded my knee,
Softly, with his Harvard degree and aftershave pieties.

I was unimpressed and afraid, withdrew, but years lie
Between us now, and I have only pity, and suspicion.
He told me then, Anglicanish, to believe that wine
Became bloody, if I wanted it to. That is desire,

Not theology. But sex is the cruellest transubstantiation.
It changes everything, or little else, or nothing at all.
His fall was just a minor infraction in the list of atrocities;
I walk, empty-handed, the bread shop sells no bread,

Is only a front for a laundromat for money. It vends OK
Flat whites, in small white paper cups, like dentists use
For the spitting system. I mutter a dismal hymn,
I snap selfies under pinking blossoms. It's spring, but

Not in Tokyo or Paris. It's riotously divided London;
Knifed apart by the rise of an economics of cruelty;
They say there's violence in anything that moves;
There's a certain Eros in writing that kills with gloves;

A strangling pressure on the breath-taking disciples;
Words are utterances from an evil presence, or love,
Or in truth, both, for love is evil and good, as the Brontë's
Testified to. I am lacking a discipline or few; I'm chilly

In the cool sun. A stabber could come up from behind,
I'd not see my own immediate decline from older chump
To emptying heart pump. My beloved is younger,
Uncertain and concerned, and so much is left to earn;

Many jokes to be badly turned on the tragedian's lathe;
We bathe in the blood and milk of human ingenuity,
And mathematicians' paperbacks. We're saturated
In superannuation and schedules of other's devising;

We're divination's little sister, the sage of a smaller location;
The oracle with a broken lens, many clicks from Delphi.
I mean, this day's wanderings are not those of Ossian, Orion,
Or the comical fakeries of the Onion. It's just an opinion,

But the trees are dividing, and the doors have unlocked,
Carry in their flaming branches a breaking parliament.
I had not meant to be political merely lyrical in my song,
Still, it is apposite, since I have been outside for so long.

April 1, 2019

ON LEARNING OF THE MURDER OF
MANOLIS FOUR YEARS LATER

What to do with this?
He was the taverna owner
On the island we honeymooned on.
He'd stand behind the counter, show us the fish;

I recall his wife more, she'd bring us our retsina, the bill.
They had a bunch of boys, all nice lads, who brought the bread.
We'd sit on the terrace, above their home, dream of moving there.
Every time we came back to Hydra, we'd seek them out, return

For the welcome, the freshness. I read now they were
Tied up by five men, the married couple, and he was
Tortured to tell them where the jewels and money
Hid. I didn't know about any other fortune

Beyond their friends, family, good food.
Manolis died, she survived.
There is evil in this.
I move from shape, form, language,

Plan revenge - but that's useless.
I have no skills in that department,
And we know killing never resurrects.
My eloquence terminates at the harbour,

Deepens into inconsequence.
It's part of the awful
Dishing out of undeserved fates
I've gained experience of

In this conflicted space.
Tragic is a word over-used, and incorrectly.
The tragic bring their deaths upon themselves
With actions - or was it wrong to hide wealth?

Was it gossip, hubris?
Who first heard the rumours,
Who spread the ugly fire?
I'd sooner have heard the island entire

Had been sunk, a new Atlantis
Than lose Manolis. Poor Manolis.
Rich Manolis.
Oh Christina, hear my prayers, I am incapable

Of bringing god's grace to your table,
I bear nothing, a poet's supper;
What sort of cook can only stare at the raw meat
Of suffering, and leave it cold, and bare?

I'd lie this cruelty into fiction, a rough movie
To thrill the ravenous mob we're all part of;
I'd call it true crime, but then erase
The Podcast before the time.

I'm the opposite of time, the pilot
Whose hull's been rammed; the houses of light
Are dimmed, have gone down.
It's all a tangled sea, stabbed by accident, screams.

The drowning sailors wake into filling lungs;
There's a clarity in dying
Never grasped in dreams.
My elegy is beaten by Tennyson's.

Love rises about as high as the sun;
Then sinks below the body's horizon;
We can breathe only so much empyrean;
Mostly we're sublunar, submergent.

It's urgent I make this beautiful, justice
Likes elegance, pretty bows.
No present is worthy of a massacre.
Tortured? How? As Jesu' was.

I knew their souls, briefly met them,
They had a radiance, modest divinity.
To be torn apart in the wood by a frenzy,
A curse of the gods.

Poetry can only circle, there's no landing
To bring murder to ground.
It stains the air, hangs like a rude flag
On a ship of stench,

Holed and listing, its hold of bones
Weighing nothing less than their sons.
Oh, human family, it's you
That's been chair-bound here.

The dumb nastiness of incivility
Eats my liver, then my heart.
The white Venetian marble glows.
The town emits a purity.

Under the gazeless sky unpity hits out,
Pelting the wedding couple running
Young and drenched from the rain;
Her dress stuck to her skin.

June 7, 2019

TODD SWIFT

was born on Good Friday in 1966, in Montreal,
Canada, and is the author of over ten full collections of poetry, and
numerous pamphlets. He published his first poems in the late 1980s,
and has edited many international anthologies, the first in 1988, as
well as being the publisher of dozens of books, as director of Eyewear
Publishing. In 2017-2018 he was for a year the Poet-in-residence
at Pembroke College, Cambridge. His PhD is on modern British
poetry's style, from the UEA. He lives in London, England, with
his wife. He now holds British and Canadian citizenship.
In 2019, he was one of three poets nominated
for the role of Oxford Professor of Poetry.

Thank you to Edwin Smet,
who designed this, and Patrick Chapman,
who read an earlier version. Also, thank you to all the friends,
and muses, real and imaginary, who helped inspire this work.
Thank you to the doctors who administer to my mind and soul,
and my friend, Fr. Brennan, who does so, too.
Thank you, MJ Penny!

As always, thank you,
to my wife, Sara Egan,
my fairest friend and guide.

Lightning Source UK Ltd.
Milton Keynes UK
UKHW012300110919
349608UK00004B/371/P